USS PAMPANITO

A Submarine and Her Crew

Carl Nolte

SAN FRANCISCO MARITIME NATIONAL PARK ASSOCIATION

Library of Congress Catalog Card Number 2001095812
ISBN 0-9714550-0-7

Editor: Kathryn M. Eustis
Designer: Jamison Spittler/Jamison Design
Technical Illustrator: Kwong Liew
Artifact Photographer: Elisabeth Fall
Fact Checking and Captions: Tom Richardson and Aldona Sendzikas
Editorial Consultant: Susan Tasaki

Printed on recycled paper in Hong Kong through Global Interprint, Inc.

The San Francisco Maritime National Park Association was established in 1950 to preserve the maritime history of the West Coast and to encourage public appreciation of our rich maritime heritage. The Association is the not-for-profit partner of San Francisco Maritime National Historical Park and supports the Park through the management of educational programs, preservation projects, volunteer recruitment, legislative advocacy and retail sales. The Association independently manages the restored World War II submarine USS *Pampanito*, which serves as a learning lab for school children, a unique public museum of history and technology, and a memorial to World War II submarine veterans. Proceeds from admissions, sales and tuition support the Association's mission: "bringing maritime history to life."

Right: WARTIME SHEET MUSIC INSPIRED BY SUBMARINE SKIPPER COMMANDER HOWARD W. GILMORE, 1943. "Take her down!" was the fateful command issued by Gilmore as he lay wounded on the bridge of his submarine, the USS *Growler* (SS-215), during an encounter with an enemy patrol vessel. For giving up his life to save his ship and crew, Gilmore became the first submariner to be awarded the Congressional Medal of Honor. (SFMNPA Collection)

Front flap, detail: The restored World War II submarine USS *Pampanito*, open daily to the public at Pier 45 in San Francisco, CA. (David Allen Photography)

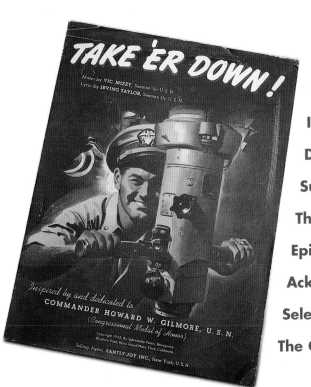

Contents

PAMPANITO'S BATTLEFLAG. The *Pampanito*'s battleflag reflects her wartime achievements. The red hash marks indicate her six war patrols; the red sun flags stand for six merchant vessels sunk and four damaged; and the red cross symbolizes the seventy-three prisoners of war rescued. (SFMNPA Collection)

Introduction

Riding easily on the blue green waters of San Francisco Bay, not far from the restaurants and tourist attractions of Fisherman's Wharf, is the gray World War II U.S. Navy submarine *Pampanito*, a memorial to another time and place.

The United States Ship *Pampanito* made 697 dives during her career. She went out on six war patrols, prowled the seas as a hunter and a killer, sank six ships and damaged four others, and rescued seventy-three men who had been left to die by a cruel enemy in a drama Admiral Chester Nimitz called "one of the most sensational stories of the war."

The *Pampanito* is a carefully preserved memorial; she looks and feels as if the crew has just left her: young men who had volunteered to sail out to the far Pacific to live alongside machinery, to sleep atop torpedoes, and to face death under the ocean. She is a memorial to those who served aboard submarines and came home to tell about it. She is also a memorial to the fifty-two American submarines and their crews that sailed to war and never returned.

This is the *Pampanito*'s story.

Dive!

Imagine yourself in this situation: It is Easter weekend. The grass is green at home, and there are spring flowers. You are a young man, serving in the submarine *Pampanito*, in the Pacific, not far from Guam, in enemy waters, thousands of miles from home. By day the ocean is flat calm. At night the moon rises just after seven. Your submarine's job is to kill anything you see because it is the enemy. The enemy's job is to kill you.

The *Pampanito* is a new boat. This is your first patrol and you are the hunter. It is April 1944.

The sonar man picks up the sounds of ships at half-past noon. Then, through the periscope, on the horizon, the skipper sees a small freighter, trailing a plume of black smoke. Lieutenant Commander Pete Summers dives deep, brings the *Pampanito* back to periscope depth and sees what he's looking for: a convoy of Japanese merchant ships, heading southwest. At 1:30 p.m., just an hour after the convoy was first sighted, Summers lines up to fire torpedoes. At the last second, he swings the periscope around to make sure everything is clear—and sees a Japanese destroyer escort bearing down, not a quarter of a mile away, right there, white foam curling from her bow. "Take her deep," Summers snaps. The hunter is now the hunted.

Aboard the *Pampanito*, diving to get away that Easter weekend in 1944, the crew knew the prey had turned on them, knew that the Japanese warship would try to kill them. The ship passed overhead at first. They heard the high-speed screw propellers, a kind of swish-swish-swish sound, very loud. Then, nothing.

"It's the waiting. To get the experience of a depth charge, you gotta be there," said Bud Arcement, an electrician's mate who was there. "It's not like the movies."

USS *Pampanito* pictured in San Francisco Bay, July 1945, immediately following her major overhaul at Hunters Point Navy Yard. (U.S. Navy photograph)

When you are young, you feel immortal. Not then. Death was very near, right above. "We said our prayers," an officer said.

That Friday the enemy warships worked the *Pampanito* over for what seemed like forever—about two hours. The *Pampanito* crept away safely, and the convoy steamed off. The sub stayed down by day and followed on the surface by night. It took all weekend. It seemed the enemy had gotten away.

Finally, at nearly 3:30 Monday morning, the radar picked up another convoy: six ships, zig-zagging. It looked like two big ships with four warship escorts. The *Pampanito* spent all day chasing it; no sleep. At 10:00 that night, the submarine attacked again, fired at and hit a ship, but again, the tables were turned. This time it was two Japanese destroyers; and again, the skip-per took the *Pampanito* down.

When the submarine was rigged to withstand depth charges, all the watertight doors were dogged down, which meant that no one could go from one part of the vessel to another. The lit-tle world of the submarine was now nine tiny worlds. "If you are in a compartment, and the doors are closed, you become a member of that compartment," said a radio technician. On a sub, everybody has to know everyone else's job.

Now the depth charging began. "There was a sound of a detonator," said Roger Walters, the sonar man who first heard the ships. "Like a click. Click, then BOOM. You hear that, and you know they are very close."

The crew could hear the sound of depth charges going in the water and the screws of the ship going over them, the whirring of the propellers and then WHAM! It was something you never forget. Never.

Summers had ordered the sub down to 450 feet, but she kept going down, and down, deeper than 450 feet, down, tilting by the stern. It felt like the angle was about seventeen degrees. Six hundred feet was crush depth, so they were told. The pressure on the hull was tremendous: twenty tons per square foot. And the depth charging went on.

Some light fixtures broke, and the glass on some of the gauges broke. Everything shook; the air was full of dust from the hull's cork insulation.

"We were hurting," another man said. "You get to where you don't have a big margin. Some of the gaskets that sealed off the air induction for the diesel engines must have worked loose from the pounding or the pressure, and the intakes filled with water." There was a steady whine, loud, terrifying, like the devil was outside, trying to get in.

It was a terrible, steady noise. "The biggest damn noise you ever heard," an officer remembered, "and we were trying to run silent."

Up above, the Japanese sound men were listening for the sub; down below, the crew of the *Pampanito* could hear the sonar, pinging, searching for them.

It was tough to take. "On the first patrol, we had a guy going goofy," said Arcement. "He was foaming at the mouth. He wanted off—right NOW. I hit him. Knocked him down. You had to."

One guy got so scared he went to the bottom bunk in the after torpedo room to get away from the depth charges. The man wanted to get as far away as he could, but that meant nothing. If the *Pampanito* sank, they'd all die. That man was a big talker later. But not then.

The men smoked, some of them up to three packs a day. But the air got so bad that day their cigarettes wouldn't burn.

The depth charging finally stopped, and it was quiet. After midnight, they took her up, slowly at first, then faster and faster, almost uncontrolled. If the Japanese destroyers were still there, playing a trick, the *Pampanito* would be a sitting duck.

The submarine surfaced and the men came boiling up out of the hatch to man the deck guns. The moon was shining, but the ocean was empty. They had survived.

"There is a special bond," Walters said. And they'd do it again if they had to. "We would. But I just hope we don't have another war."

SUBMARINES AND TARGETS

One of the great mysteries of submarines, even to other sailors, is how a sub dives. Actually, the principle is fairly simple. A piece of wood has a density lower than that of seawater, so it floats. A brick is denser than seawater, so it sinks.

When a submarine is on the surface, it has air in its ballast tanks, which are outside the main, or pressure, hull. This situation is called positive buoyancy. To submerge, the air is released by opening a vent. As air escapes, water flows into the tank through an opening called a flood port. This creates negative buoyancy. Since the boat is now heavier than the water it displaces, it begins to descend below the surface. Sets of planes, which look like wings, or fins on a fish, control the angle of descent.

In physics, the natural law of buoyancy means that a floating body sinks until its own weight is equal to the weight of the amount of water it displaces. A submarine can get into a state of approximate neutral buoyancy—between floating and sinking—when it displaces its own weight of water. Blowing air back into one of the water-filled ballast tanks—the Negative Tank—halts descent. Once the sub is in approximate neutral buoyancy, planes on the sides of the boat control its depth.

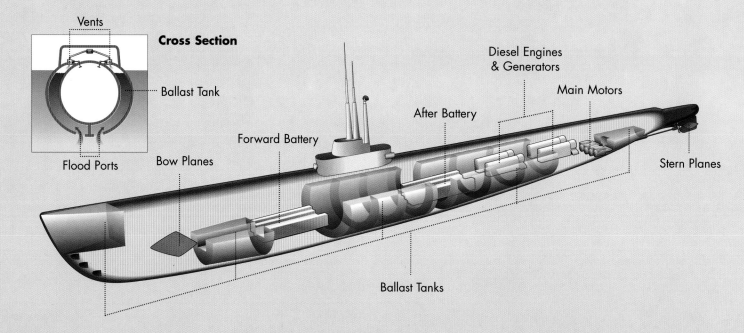

Vents

Cross Section

Ballast Tank

Flood Ports

Bow Planes

Forward Battery

After Battery

Diesel Engines & Generators

Main Motors

Stern Planes

Ballast Tanks

To surface, compressed air carried on board is blown into the tanks, forcing the water out and making the boat lighter than the water it displaces. The angle of ascent can also be controlled by the bow and stern planes.

Balao class fleet submarines are powered by four diesel engines connected to generators that supply electricity to electric motors; this is called diesel-electric drive. When on the surface, the diesels turn the generators. But the diesels, which breathe air, cannot run submerged. So underwater, the electric motors are powered by batteries.

The *Pampanito* and boats like her could make 20 knots and more on the surface but only up to 10 knots submerged. On the surface, the submarine had a range of about 22,000 miles per patrol, but submerged, the range was about 95 miles at a time—a little more than the distance from San Francisco to Sacramento. This is because the electric batteries could be used for only a matter of hours before needing to be recharged—and the only way to charge the batteries was to run the diesel engines. This meant that these silent underwater killers had to become surface vessels—vulnerable to air and sea attacks. An enemy catching a sub on the surface has won half the battle.

American boats were not equipped with snorkels, the underwater breathing devices used by later German U-boats. Diesel boats then were not true submarines, since they could not stay down indefinitely. The first true submarines ran on nuclear energy, which provided so much power that subs could make their own oxygen and stay underwater for months.

During World War II, American submarines had several advantages over other subs. For one thing, they had good radar. There were four kinds of radar: the SD radar, a low-frequency device, detected planes; the SV radar was also an air-search radar; the SJ radar, mounted forward of the SD antenna, swept the surface of the ocean to detect ships; and the ST radar was built into one of the two periscopes. Radar was a British invention, manufactured at high volume and high quality by American industry. American radar

EASTMAN-KODAK MARK I SUBMARINE PERISCOPE CAMERA. The Mark I was a standard 35-mm Kodak still-picture camera, adapted for naval use through the addition of a high-tech viewfinder that enabled the user to view the target through the periscope while the photo was being taken. (SFMNPA Collection)

was high tech for its time, far superior to anything the Japanese had.

American boats also had the TDC, the torpedo data computer. The TDC could determine the gyro angle of a torpedo fired at a target. The problem was very much like a football quarterback trying to throw a ball to a receiver. A quarterback makes all the computations—angle, speed, and direction—in his head. On a submarine, the observations of the target, the bearing, and the estimated speed were made by the officer in charge of the attack. The actual computations for setting the gyroscope angle for the course of the torpedo were made in the TDC and transmitted to the torpedo room. It was a complex set of factors that combined mechanics and human judgment. If it was correct, the torpedo hit the target ship.

There is a saying among submariners: There are only two kinds of ships—submarines and targets.

The USS *Pampanito* underwent a major overhaul at San Francisco's Hunters Point Navy Yard in 1945. The circled items in this official Navy photograph indicate new or modified equipment. The newly installed SV radar mast can be seen here. (U.S. Navy photograph)

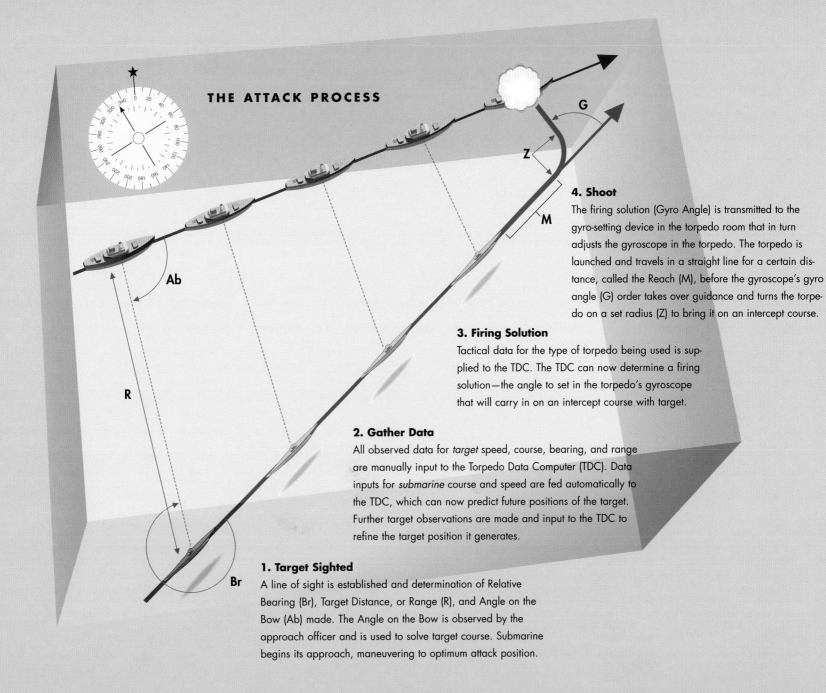

THE ATTACK PROCESS

4. Shoot

The firing solution (Gyro Angle) is transmitted to the gyro-setting device in the torpedo room that in turn adjusts the gyroscope in the torpedo. The torpedo is launched and travels in a straight line for a certain distance, called the Reach (M), before the gyroscope's gyro angle (G) order takes over guidance and turns the torpedo on a set radius (Z) to bring it on an intercept course.

3. Firing Solution

Tactical data for the type of torpedo being used is supplied to the TDC. The TDC can now determine a firing solution—the angle to set in the torpedo's gyroscope that will carry in on an intercept course with target.

2. Gather Data

All observed data for *target* speed, course, bearing, and range are manually input to the Torpedo Data Computer (TDC). Data inputs for *submarine* course and speed are fed automatically to the TDC, which can now predict future positions of the target. Further target observations are made and input to the TDC to refine the target position it generates.

1. Target Sighted

A line of sight is established and determination of Relative Bearing (Br), Target Distance, or Range (R), and Angle on the Bow (Ab) made. The Angle on the Bow is observed by the approach officer and is used to solve target course. Submarine begins its approach, maneuvering to optimum attack position.

BNP 672
(Revised Sept. 1942)

The United States of America

Navy Department ⚓ Bureau of Naval Personnel

Navy Training Course Certificate

BOURGEOIS, Roger Norman, #666-07-13, MoMM2c, V-6, USNR.

having completed the Navy Training Course

MOTOR MACHINIST'S MATE FIRST CLASS AND CHIEF MOTOR MACHINIST'S MATE

with a mark of 3.74 **, is awarded this certificate this** 1st

day of APRIL **, 19** 45 **Notation to this effect has been made in his service record.**

P. E. Summers

T. N. SWAIN,   P. E. SUMMERS,

Lieutenant, **U. S. Navy,**   Commander, **U. S. Navy,**
Division Officer.   **Commanding**
                              U. S. S. PAMPANITO (SS383)

Submarine Service

Submarines are the perfect weapon—deadly, powerful, and nearly invisible. Submarines can strike and then vanish. Today's nuclear submarines can sail around the world under the ocean; they can creep under the pack ice to the North Pole. During World War II, German submarines were so powerful that they nearly brought Great Britain to defeat, and American submarines were so well handled that they cost Japan its empire.

In the long twilight struggle of the Cold War, nuclear submarines prowled the oceans of the world, ready to crush any enemy. Submarines are still on patrol in the deep, waiting, ready for anything.

Submarine sailors are a special breed—an elite force of volunteers who live, and sometimes die, in a steel tube that sails under the ocean. Much of what they do is secret. During World War II, war correspondents were almost never allowed on submarines, and submarine sailors—members of what one writer called "the tightest of closed societies"—did not talk about what they did. Submarine service came to be called The Silent Service.

Even today, life on a submarine is a bit of a mystery. "People have no concept of how a submarine works or what it's like to live on one," said George Moffett, who served as a radio technician on the *Pampanito* during wartime.

Left: NAVY TRAINING COURSE CERTIFICATE. Issued to *Pampanito* crew member Roger Bourgeois for having successfully completed motor machinist's mate training. The certificate is dated April 1945 and is signed by two of the *Pampanito*'s officers, indicating that the training was probably completed on board. (SFMNPA Collection)

Above: RECRUITING BOOKLET ISSUED BY THE U.S. NAVY IN 1944. In addition to historical facts about the submarine, this booklet contains information about life on board and assurances of the many opportunities for advancement available in the Submarine Service, as well as an inspiring "Submariner's Creed." (SFMNPA Collection)

The first submarine was invented in 1620 by a Dutchman named Cornelius Van Drebbel, a doctor at the court of King James I of England. Van Drebbel built a submarine powered by oars, which submerged in the River Thames and sailed underwater from Westminster to Greenwich though the heart of London, a feat witnessed by the king himself.

A submarine was first used as a weapon in the American Revolution. On September 6, 1776, only two months after the United States proclaimed its independence, a submarine named *Turtle* attacked the British warship HMS *Eagle* in New York Harbor.

Submarines were also used in the American Civil War. The first ship ever sunk by a submarine was the USS *Housatonic*, which was sent to the bottom by the Confederate Navy submarine *H.L. Hunley* in February 1864. The attack was fatal to both vessels, but the *Hunley* came to the surface again 136 years later when her hull was salvaged from the harbor in Charleston, South Carolina.

The U.S. Navy's first submarine was the USS *Holland*, named after her inventor and commissioned in 1900. It was such a success that the Navy ordered four more.

But it was the Germans who, during World War I, showed the real power of the submarine as a weapon. The German vessels—called *unterseeboote*, or U-boats—sank 18.7 million tons of Allied shipping and nearly brought Britain to defeat. Instead, Germany's tactics of unrestricted submarine warfare (sinking merchant ships without warning) brought the United States into the war and ensured Germany's defeat.

They called World War I "the war to end all wars," and the submarine was a symbol of the worst of warfare. "To those outside the [submarine] service, the U-boat campaign against merchant shipping had given the submarine a reprehensible image. By war's end it was almost universally loathed," wrote Clair Blair, Jr. in his classic book *Silent Victory*. "Many notable persons in both Europe and the United States argued the submarine was immoral, and, like poison gas, should be outlawed."

Rather than being outlawed, the submarine proved that it was among the handful of powerful weapons that could, by themselves, tip the scales toward victory.

The Germans almost proved it again in World War II when their U-boats, this time acting in "wolf-packs," nearly cut off the British Isles. Of all the weapons the Nazis arrayed against Britain, Winston Churchill said he feared the U-boat most.

Churchill became prime minister in 1940, the year the Germans overran western Europe and left Britain alone to face the Nazi war machine. The island nation had to be supplied by sea in order to fight the war. The German tactic was to sink ships faster than they could be replaced. The idea was to starve out the British before the immense power of the United States could be brought to bear; the weapon was the submarine.

The Allies responded by sending ships in heavily protected convoys and using planes and warships to hunt down the U-boats. The Germans eventually lost the Battle of the Atlantic.

But in a similar situation on the other side of the world, the Americans succeeded where the Germans had failed. And the weapon the Americans used was the submarine.

At first, the war at sea went badly for the Allies in the Pacific. The Japanese surprised the United States fleet at Pearl Harbor, ran the British out of Malaya and Singapore, invaded and captured the Philippines, overran Indonesia and Thailand, and sank nearly every warship the Allies sent against them. In six months, Japan had captured a huge Far Eastern empire and in so doing secured all the raw materials they needed for a world war—oil, tin, rubber, bauxite to make aluminum, and rice to feed a warrior nation. But the huge Japanese Empire had within it a fatal flaw. All the materials needed in Japan had to arrive by sea. Japan, too, is an island country.

"No major power in the world was more dependent on ocean shipping than Japan," a U.S. commission reported after the war.

In the beginning, American submarines were hampered by poorly designed torpedoes and what historians called "the skipper problem"—submarine captains who were too cautious. In the first six months of the war, U.S. submarines sank only 35 Japanese merchant ships, fewer vessels than the German U-boats sank in a single month.

Then a new COMSUBPAC (Commander Submarine Force, Pacific Fleet) took over. He raged at the Navy brass until the torpedo problem was solved. He replaced nearly a third of his sub captains. His name was Rear Admiral Charles A. Lockwood. His submariners called him Uncle Charlie—but not to his face.

Soon new submarines like the *Pampanito* came on stream, fast, sophisticated boats built quickly in the United States and equipped with the best American technology: radar, computers to aim torpedoes, and the best array of surface weapons of any submarines afloat. They were only 311 feet long, about the size of a medium ferryboat. They carried twenty-four torpedoes and a crew of up to ninety officers and men, all volunteers.

At the beginning of World War II, Japan had 2,337 merchant ships. By the end of the war, only 231 were left. The rest had been sunk. Submarines alone sank sixty percent of Japan's merchant

WARTIME SHEET MUSIC INSPIRED BY SUBMARINE SKIPPER COMMANDER HOWARD W. GILMORE, 1943. "Take her down!" was the fateful command issued by Gilmore as he lay wounded on the bridge of his submarine, the USS *Growler*, during an encounter with an enemy ship. (SFMNPA Collection)

fleet and a total of 1,314 Japanese ships, including 1 battleship, 8 aircraft carriers, 11 cruisers, and more than 30 destroyers. The huge new aircraft carrier *Shinano* was sunk on her maiden voyage by the submarine *Archerfish* within sight of Japan's home islands. Though the popular image of the war was a navy of mighty battleships, cruisers, and fast destroyers, submarines sank twice as many enemy warships as did surface vessels.

By the end of 1944, when the *Pampanito* and her sisters were prowling the approaches to Japan, the Japanese government ran short of everything from aviation fuel to materials for building planes. They launched an emergency program to distill aviation fuel from potatoes. Japan had virtually no reserves of fuel oil and no tankers could make it through the submarine-filled seas. The last convoy to bring oil from Indonesia arrived in Japan in March 1945. The Japanese Empire was coming to an end. Without oil, ships couldn't sail and without ships to bring supplies, Japan would slowly starve.

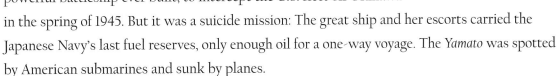

Desperate, the Imperial Navy sent the battleship *Yamato*, the most powerful battleship ever built, to intercept the U.S. fleet off Okinawa in the spring of 1945. But it was a suicide mission: The great ship and her escorts carried the Japanese Navy's last fuel reserves, only enough oil for a one-way voyage. The *Yamato* was spotted by American submarines and sunk by planes.

There was a price for this victory: The U.S. Navy lost 52 submarines, and more than 3,500 submarine sailors never returned from patrol—a death rate of twenty percent, the highest of any branch of the combat services.

PAMPANITO PATROL "CRUISOGRAPH." Issued after a successfully completed deep submergence test, this commemorative illustration probably dates to July 1945, after the *Pampanito*'s refit at Hunters Point. (SFMNPA Collection)

EARLY FAILURES

When American submarines joined the war, they fought with two huge handicaps. The first was mechanical and the second was human.

The primary weapon of a submarine, of course, is the torpedo, fired from the submarines at "targets," as all other vessels are called. Most United States submarines were armed with Mark 14 torpedoes, which carried up to 643 pounds of high explosive and were powered by miniature steam turbines. The Mark 14 torpedoes were complex killing machines, at least in theory.

But they had never been properly tested—and never used in combat. It turned out that the torpedoes ran about ten feet deeper than they were set to run—and went right under the ships they were supposed to hit. Even after that problem was fixed, it was discovered that the American torpedoes also had faulty firing pins, or exploders, as the top-secret devices were called. The exploder had two different ways of operating and neither way worked 100 percent of the time—so even if a torpedo reached its target, it didn't always explode.

For these reasons, American subs got poor results in the first months of the war. The Navy brass blamed the crews, not the weapons. Many skippers got poor ratings for their patrols. One of them was Lieutenant Commander Frederick Warder, a man with such a reputation for aggressive action that he was called Fearless Freddy. His official explanation for one less-than-stellar patrol with the USS *Seawolf*: "The goddamned torpedoes were no damned good. That was the problem."

MARK XIV STEAM TORPEDO

Main Engine   Propeller Shafts
Gyro Pot
(houses gyroscope)   Depth &
Steering Rudders

WARHEAD
Contains High Explosive Charge
& Exploder Mechanism

AIR FLASK SECTION
Contains Air Compartment,
Water Compartment & Fuel Flask

AFTER BODY & TAIL SECTIONS

And it was. But it took months to convince the top admirals, months that cost many American lives. The torpedo crisis was a wartime secret—and the failure at the top to understand the problem was a scandal that was not revealed until after the war.

The second problem—that of weak and ineffective captains—is harder to assess. The submarine captain is almost a cliché out of all the old war movies: the German skipper, with his white hat on backwards, peering through a periscope at a helpless merchant ship; the handsome American captain, staring steely-eyed at an enemy warship. Each was shown as a calm, efficient, fearless man. Sometimes he was ruthless, sometimes he was just doing his job.

The truth was different. Captains were men like any other, put into jobs unlike any in the world. The submarine was, in fact, its own tiny world, and the captain was king. He made all the decisions, picked the targets to attack, and tracked them with the periscope. The rest of the crew saw the world—and life and death—through the captain's eyes. The captain bore all the responsibility for the operation of the boat, the lives of her crew, and the lives of the submarine's enemies. Nearly all of the 465 skippers who commanded U.S. submarines in combat were Naval Academy graduates. Very few were reserve officers.

Submarine commanders were picked carefully and their performance was evaluated harshly. At the beginning of the war, many captains were thought to be too cautious, unwilling to take the necessary risks. They were trained that way, some critics said, in the long period of peacetime, where caution and seniority were the paths to promotion.

But this was wartime. The pressure was always on; results were expected and excuses were not tolerated. "The truth was there was absolutely no way to tell in advance whether a new submarine skipper would be aggressive or nonaggressive," said historian Clay Blair. "What he did, how he performed, was the result of deep inner motivation that could not be quantified or assessed in port or even when he was an exec [the executive officer, or second in command].... There was only one solution to the problem: Give everybody who deserved it and was qualified a chance and see how he made out. Then, if he failed to perform, relieve him after two patrols."

Thirty percent of the skippers—nearly one in three—were relieved in 1942, fourteen percent in 1943 and fourteen percent in 1944.

Being captain of a submarine was a nearly impossible job. There was always a shortage of good captains.

MRS JAMES WOLFENDEN
CHRISTENING U.S.S. CHAMPANITAS
LAUNCHING PORTSMOUTH

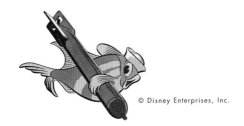

© Disney Enterprises, Inc.

The *Pampanito* and Her Times

The years always go by faster than anyone expects, and before you know what happened exactly, the young men who served aboard the *Pampanito* when the world was at war are old men, remembering.

But their memories are not faded, like old photographs. They are as sharp as the November wind that blows across San Francisco Bay and sets the USS *Pampanito* rolling at her berth. The boat is a memorial now, but what happened on that submarine cannot be forgotten, and the pull of memory, of shared experience, of affection still brings the men of the original crew back to see the submarine again.

The *Pampanito* is a memorial to another time; George Moffett lived in that time. He was a young man, a kid really, when he first saw the *Pampanito*, in the spring of 1943 at the Portsmouth Navy Yard in New Hampshire. He had a radio technician rating and was assigned to the *Pampanito*'s first crew.

Above: DISNEY LOGO. As part of their contribution to the war effort, the Walt Disney Studios provided artwork for submarine logos, including this one for the *Pampanito*. (SFMNPA Collection)

Left: Mrs. Violet Wolfenden christening the *Pampanito* on July 12, 1943, on the occasion of her double launching with sister sub *Picuda* at Portsmouth, New Hampshire. (National Archives, 80-G-73314)

The United States had been at war with Germany and Japan for more than a year, and all around the country shipyards had sprung up. Older yards like Portsmouth had been transformed. In 1940, there were 4,200 workers there. Three years later, there were five times as many. They were delivering a brand new submarine every month.

For the first time, women went to work in the shipyard. They were welders, machinists, and crane operators. The women changed the old shipyard ways. There was a war on, but everybody, it seemed, was young. There were even dances at lunchtime. Said the *Portland* (Maine) *Herald*, "Rosie the Riveter and her boyfriend [are] dancing in dungarees, munching and lunching in time to swing music that echoes in the cavernous expanse of the yard's machine shop."

PAMPANITO LOGO. Logos for the submarine were based on the small, predatory, Pacific Ocean fish after which she was named. (SFMNPA Collection)

The keel for one new boat was laid on March 15, 1943. She was launched on July 12 and christened *Pampanito* after a small brown, black, silver, and yellow fish that lives in the Pacific Ocean off Central America. On November 6, 1943, the Stars and Stripes were run up the flagstaff on the conning tower, the 48-star blue jack—symbol of a Navy ship in commission—was raised on her bow, and Lieutenant Commander Charles B. Jackson, Jr. read his orders to take command of America's newest warship, the USS *Pampanito*.

Moffett watched the boat being put together. He was more than interested; his life would depend on the workmanship in that Navy yard. "I watched them pour the brass for some of this," he said. The whole job from laying the keel to launching the vessel took just 120 days. "People can do a lot of things if they have the will to do it."

Moffett was in the *Pampanito's* first crew—in Navy parlance, he is a "plank owner"—and people like that have a special bond to each other and to the ship.

"For better or for worse, we felt 'This is our boat,' " he recalled. "You take it to sea, and you live and die with it. Every crew felt that way. They felt their boat was as good as or better than any in the fleet."

That month, the *Pampanito* went to sea for the first time. She steamed down the Piscataqua River, with Maine on the port side and New Hampshire to starboard, then out to the open Atlantic in bitter cold November weather, where she made her first dive.

The boat was brand new, and so was the crew. "Many of these guys had never seen salt water before they joined the Navy," said Seaman Second Class Gordon Hopper. "I grew up in Mason City, Iowa," said Roger Walters, who became an expert sonar man, one of the best. He had never even seen the ocean before. "I was seasick all the time. It took me six months to get over it."

Hull sections of the submarines *Pampanito* and *Picuda* being laid in the new construction basin at Portsmouth Navy Yard, March 15, 1943. These were the first two boats to be built in the new basin. (U.S. Navy photograph)

In December, the boat sailed for New London, Connecticut, then to Newport, Rhode Island, making trials and tests along the way. She went back to Portsmouth at the turn of the year, then back to Newport.

She sailed for the Panama Canal on January 15, 1944.

One of the new men aboard was George Ingram, a recruit from Philadelphia. "They told me they had a boat going to Philadelphia and did I want to go? I sure did." So he went as steward's mate in the officers' wardroom. Ingram was one of two African Americans in the crew. The next stop, to Ingram's surprise, was the Canal Zone. He used to go around saying, "Don't worry; I'm a good kid." He was a favorite of the crew, who called him Good Kid.

The *Pampanito*, Ingram thought, "had a crackerjack crew. The greatest crew in the world. I will never forget them. I wouldn't trade nothing for the experience."

It took two weeks to travel from Panama to Pearl Harbor. The *Pampanito* arrived in Hawai'i on Valentine's Day after a 4,000-mile journey.

In Pearl Harbor, Jackson was replaced as skipper by Lieutenant Commander Paul E. Summers. Summers, whose nickname was Pete, had been a starting pitcher on the Naval Academy baseball team. He was thirty years old—an old man in a crew of kids. The *Pampanito* was his first command.

Above and right: LAUNCHING TAG AND RIBBON. Issued by Portsmouth Navy Yard to commemorate the launching of the *Pampanito* and *Picuda*. Due to the speed of wartime submarine construction, double launchings such as this one were not uncommon. (SFMNPA Collection)

Right, full page: Captain C.H. Roper, USN reading orders of commissioning for the USS *Pampanito* (SS-383), November 6, 1943 at Portsmouth Navy Yard. (U.S. Navy photograph)

Right, inset: INVITATION TO THE *PAMPANITO*'S COMMISSIONING PARTY. A commissioning party for the *Pampanito*'s crew and their guests was held on October 23, 1943, two weeks before the formal commissioning ceremony. (Courtesy of Walter H. Cordon)

- 1943 -
SOUVENIR
OF
DOUBLE LAUNCHING

U. S. S. PICUDA
First-Boats-Built-in
BUILDING BASIN

U. S. S. PAMPANITO
Will soon be on her way
to avenge the sneak on
PEARL HARBOR
Dec. 7, 1941

The Officers and Crew of the U.S.S. Pampanito

request the company of

Mr. Cordon

at their Commissioning Party

October 23, 1943, from 8:00 p.m.

at Casino Del Jamon, Hams, Lafayette Road

Guest of W. Cordon E.M.L.

Please present this card at the door.

MISSIONING OF U.S.S. PAMPANITO (SS383) AT NAVY YARD, PORTSMOUTH, N.H. CAPT C.H.ROPER, U.S.N. READING THE ORDERS OF MISSIONING. NOV. 6. 1943 Neg. No. 1242-43

LIFE ABOARD

What was life aboard like? The men of the *Pampanito*'s wartime crew had good things to say. George Moffett said he actually enjoyed most of the time he spent on the *Pampanito*. Larry Noker, who had hoped to go on the submarine *Scamp*, drew the *Pampanito* instead, which saved his life. The *Scamp* was lost on her last patrol in 1944. "I thank God every day that I went on the *Pampanito*," he said.

At sea and during a war, a submarine is a cramped and noisy place, full of the smell of oil. Men are jammed together, packed in, working in heat and danger. On patrols, they were behind the enemy lines: Every ship, every plane was hostile. Yet it was also a good time, or so it seems now.

"You will notice," said Bill Bruckart, "that everybody remembers the good things. The memory of happiness is stronger than the memory of pain."

"Human nature being what it is, you like to talk about the fun parts of life," said Roger Walters. "But we have a special bond. We lived together in wartime for fifteen months."

Above: SUBMARINER'S SANDALS WORN BY TORPEDOMAN'S MATE PEDER GRANUM. Since the earliest days of the submarine service, uniform regulations on board tended to be a little lax, comfort and efficiency taking precedence over formality. On patrol in the warm Pacific waters during World War II, submariners often wore only shorts and sandals. (SFMNPA Collection)

Right: THE COOK BOOK OF THE U.S. NAVY. The submarine force claimed to serve the best food of all the branches of the military, and this 1945 cookbook, used by Ship's Cook Joseph Eichner, supports that claim. Pictured is a recipe for a favorite menu item: ice cream. Most submarines carried an ice cream maker as part of their standard galley equipment. (SFMNPA Collection)

"We were a fraternity," said Elmer Smith, "Very few people can know about battles."

"Who knows why people volunteered for submarines," said Walters. "Some felt it was the macho thing to do. It was different. It was romanticized." He paused. "It was not romantic."

"It wasn't so bad," said Harry Bowring. Soldiers and marines, he said, "had to sleep out in the rain; they had no bed. But we had all of that, we got to eat at a table and never had to worry about rain. We could take a shower every third day, if we were lucky. But some guys didn't get a shower for a couple of weeks.

"We were confined in a steel tube for two months. But we never felt confined. Time went by fast.

"Everybody had to depend on everybody else, same as a football team. If everybody works together, you win. You had to be a little crazy to go on a sub in the first place, but you had to be easy going, too. You know, where nothing would bother you. That was a big part of it. If you weren't you'd never make it. You couldn't let things bother you. You make the best of it. That's what makes a submarine man.

"We were all a bunch of crazy nuts, to tell you the truth."

If conditions permitted, a swim call allowed submariners the opportunity to take a dip in the Pacific. (Photo source unknown)

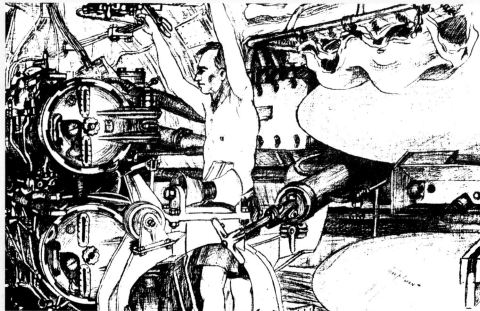

 During his service aboard the USS *Pampanito,* Gunner's Mate Tony Hauptman (pictured left) used his substantial artistic skills to create these drawings depicting his experiences on board. Subjects ranged from the routine of everyday life to the intensity of battle. (SFMNPA Collection)

The First Patrol: **Under Pressure** (March 15 to May 2, 1944)

The *Pampanito* sailed on her first patrol on March 15—a year to the day after her keel was laid. William Bruckart, who joined the boat as radar officer just before she sailed, remembers how young everybody was. "All those bright young faces. There is a hell of a difference in the willingness to suffer discomfort and daring when you are eighteen or twenty years old.

"They did it because they were young, because they wanted to do it, and because they could do it. You put the cautious guys on a battleship, the middle guys on a destroyer, and the wildcats on a submarine," Bruckart said. Most of the crew were teenagers. Bruckart himself was a lieutenant junior grade. He was twenty-three.

Bill Grady, who was also twenty-three, was a veteran; he'd spent five years in the Navy, had served on two other submarines, and had made six war patrols. He was a motor machinist's mate first class—a "motor mac" as they were called in the Navy. With submarine pay and all, he risked his life for $226 a month. "I was thrilled to go," he said.

On the first patrol, the *Pampanito* was sent to the Caroline Islands, close in to the island of Yap, on the far side of the world from the Atlantic coast.

Her mission was to provide "lifeguard" patrol: to pick up any U.S.

"IMPERIAL DOMAIN OF THE GOLDEN DRAGON" CERTIFICATE AND CARD. These commemorative items were issued to crew members when they crossed the International Date Line (the 180th Meridian) for the first time. Such ceremonies boosted morale and broke up the monotony of a long patrol at sea. (SFMNPA Collection)

fliers who had been shot down or ditched at sea. During the Pacific war, 504 aviators were rescued in this manner. It was a game of skill and mostly luck, but the *Pampanito* never picked up any fliers.

After some days, they were told to move toward Guam, and there, on April 7, 1944—Good Friday—the *Pampanito* encountered her first Japanese convoy.

Summers brought the boat to periscope depth and set up for a shot. Radioman Third Class Roger Walters was in the forward torpedo room, working the sound gear. "I was told the skipper turned the periscope aft, and all he could see was the bow wave of a ship heading right for us." It was a Japanese destroyer escort; there were two of them, and now the *Pampanito* had to dive deep for her very life. The cat and mouse game went on for hours and the convoy got away.

In the small hours of Easter Sunday, radar picked up another convoy and the *Pampanito* spent all day chasing it, lined up a shot, and fired torpedoes at one of the targets. But the attack brought on another attack by the convoy escorts and again, the *Pampanito* had to dive—down, down. She went well below her 400-foot test depth. She went down to 600 feet. Some thought she went to 650 feet. "When the light fixtures are breaking . . . you know you are being worked over," recalled one of the crew. "That was scary. They were all scary."

But the Japanese destroyers finally moved off and the *Pampanito* was able to surface just after midnight. The boat had been damaged but she could be repaired.

She went back on patrol, was harassed with bombs from enemy planes on occasion but escaped these encounters undamaged. Now seriously short of fuel, the sub was sent to Midway

PATROL REPORT: MARCH 19, 1944

0800–1200 Underway as before.

0800 Mustered crew on stations; no absentees.

0825 Changed base course to 277° T.

0855 Dived.

0900 Surfaced.

0905 Dived.

0911 Surfaced.

0915 Dived.

0920 Surfaced.

0923 Dived.

0928 Surfaced.

0933 Went ahead at standard speed on 2 main engines on base course 277° T.

1000 Made daily visual inspection of magazines and smokeless powder samples; conditions normal. (0838 Crossed the International Date Line at latitude 18° 19′ North and changed date to 20 March 1944.)

Right, full page: The Royal Hawaiian Hotel. (Photo source unknown)

Right, insets: ROYAL HAWAIIAN RETURN PASS. The famous Royal Hawaiian Hotel on Waikiki Beach, known as the Pink Palace, was taken over by the military during the war for use as an R&R facility for submariners and aviators. Enlisted men paid twenty-five cents a day and stayed four to a room; still, compared to "hotbunking" on a submarine, it was luxurious. (SFMNPA Collection)
CHOW PASS. Issued to Torpedoman's Mate Elmer W. Smith for access to the mess hall on the Pearl Harbor Submarine Base. (SFMNPA Collection)

Below: A group of young *Pampanito* crewmen posing in Hawai'i between patrols. (Courtesy of Roger Bourgeois, SFMNPA Collection)

Below right: CREW MEMBER'S BIBLE. Pocket-sized New Testament Bible with steel cover, carried on board the *Pampanito* by Chief Radioman Mervin Hill, who served on all six of the submarine's war patrols. (SFMNPA Collection)

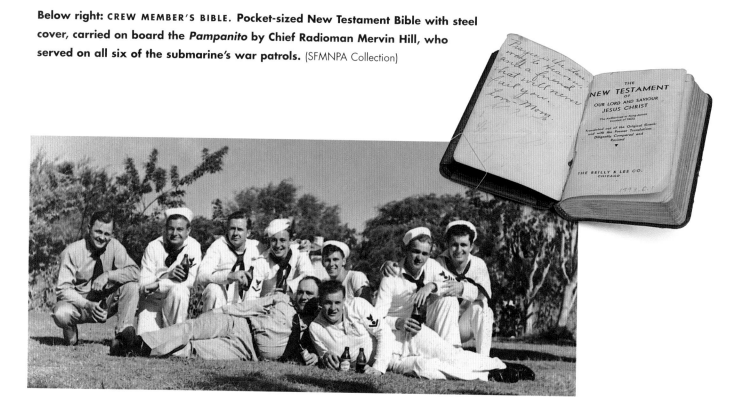

Island. She arrived with fuel tanks nearly empty—practically running the diesels on fumes. She then went to Pearl Harbor for repairs and an overhaul.

And the men got a break: two weeks' rest and recuperation at the famous Royal Hawaiian Hotel, right in Waikiki.

The Second Patrol: **Dangerous Waters** (June 3 to July 23, 1944)

The *Pampanito* sailed from Pearl Harbor for Midway on June 3; she spent about a day on Midway and then sailed west on June 8. Summers opened his sealed orders: The boat was being sent to the coast of Japan itself to patrol in an area called The Hit Parade, after the stateside radio show.

In mid-June, the *Pampanito* ran into a typhoon with huge seas as she closed in on the Japanese coast. She reached a series of small islands off Kyushu; then, on the first days of summer, the famous Bungo Strait—the entrance to Japan's Inland Sea, one of the most dangerous places in the world for American submarines.

The summer seas off Japan are famous for their phosphorescence. When a ship moves in the water, it disturbs thousands of tiny plankton, and they glow silver. "You'd be amazed," said George Moffett. "Everything that moves leaves a phosphorescent wake, just like an arrow, pointing at you."

Above: *Pampanito* crew members sharing a lighter moment during a break at Midway Island. (Photo source unknown)

Right, full page: *Pampanito* tied up to the tender (supply vessel) USS *Proteus* at Midway in May 1944. The smiles on the crew belie the harrowing adventures they experienced on their first patrol. (Photo source unknown)

Right, inset: GOONEYVILLE CARD. Sailors who pulled into Midway Island between patrols called it "Gooneyville" because one of the only things to do was to watch the clumsy take-offs and landings of the resident gooney birds (a type of albatross). (SFMNPA Collection)

Guest of
GOONEYVILLE
From the
USS *Rampanito* 221
(NOTE TO HOLDER)
This identification card is your admission
ticket to the Mess and Beer Halls
DON'T LOSE IT—NO ADMISSION WITHOUT IT

Electrician's Mate Paul Pappas (pictured far right) kept his personal camera, a Rolleicord, with him while serving on the *Pampanito*—a violation of the rule against such cameras aboard American submarines. He used it to photograph other members of the crew. With the blessing of the skipper, he brought out his camera and recorded the dramatic rescue of British and Australian prisoners of war from the South China Sea during the third war patrol (see page 41). (Courtesy of Paul Pappas, SFMNPA Collection)

SECRETS

It was called The Silent Service for a reason. Not only did submarines operate under the ocean, by stealth and in the dark, they sailed with secret orders and with secret advantages.

One advantage was the depth to which they could dive. Originally, fleet submarines—boats designed so they could sail fast enough to keep up with the Navy's surface fleet in all weather—had an operating depth of 300 feet. But toward the end of 1941, two submarine design officers, one from the Portsmouth Navy Yard and one from the Bureau of Ships, got together and made some calculations on the back of an envelope. They figured that if the thickness of the steel hull plating on the *Gato* class boats could be increased from nine-sixteenths to seven-eighths of an inch, the hulls would be capable of withstanding submergence to 925 feet.

To provide a margin of safety, operating depth was set at 400 feet. These new thicker-skinned submarines were designated *Balao* class, named for the first boat of the class (the *Pampanito* is a *Balao* class boat). The new thicker skins of the *Balao* class, and the boats' ability to dive much deeper than previous submarines, were kept secret. If the enemy knew how deep a sub could dive, they would know how deep to set their depth charges.

On the *Pampanito*'s first patrol, the boat dived to 650 feet—250 feet deeper than test depth—while under attack by Japanese warships. The capacity to dive deep probably saved the *Pampanito*.

Balao class submarines were a wartime evolution of the fleet-type submarine. They had thicker hulls than the preceding *Gato* class, allowing them to dive about 100 feet deeper to elude the enemy. Crewman Paul Pappas can be seen here posing on the stern plane while the *Pampanito* lays in drydock. (Courtesy of Paul Pappas, SFMNPA Collection)

On the port side of the *Pampanito*, just forward of the galley where the crew's meals were cooked, was a tiny radio room, and in it, right next to the boat's main passageway, was a code machine—and another secret.

Incoming radio messages on the sub were in the dots and dashes of Morse Code, received in random five-letter coded groups—a code within a code. Sometimes the message was in what the U.S. Navy called ULTRA—a secret message for the captain's eyes only. Those ULTRA messages were the deepest and darkest secrets of the war because the Allies had cracked the German and Japanese codes, and the enemy didn't know it. The Germans and Japanese kept sending supposedly secret messages—plans, orders, positions of warships, all kinds of information—in codes that had been broken, and the U.S. Navy relayed that information to its officers in the field using ULTRA.

The British had cracked the German code after they captured an Enigma code machine intact from a disabled U-boat. It was a tremendous break. But the Americans learned to read secret Japanese messages by the pure brainpower of a team of cryptologists, who deciphered the code used by the Japanese diplomatic service—the so-called Purple Code—in 1940. The military code took longer, but by the spring of 1942, the United States Navy could read eighty-five percent of Japan's naval codes.

ELECTRONIC CIPHER MACHINE (ECM) MARK II. Used aboard submarines during World War II to encipher messages from plain text into code, and from code back into ordinary text. This ECM, currently exhibited in *Pampanito*'s radio room, is on loan from the U.S. Naval Security Group and is believed to be the only fully operable ECM Mark II in existence. (Courtesy of U.S. Naval Security Group)

The U.S.'s success at the battle of Midway was the most famous result of this effort. Armed with knowledge of Japan's strategy, the U.S. Navy surprised the Imperial Navy at Midway and achieved the greatest naval victory in history, a turning point of the war in the Pacific.

ULTRA was a key weapon in the war under the seas. The Japanese were careful planners; they sent ships to sea with specific instructions. Since these instructions could be decoded by U.S. military intelligence, U.S. commanders knew how many ships were in a convoy and their estimated daily noon positions, and could plot the course and speed of the ships.

This information was key to the interception of Japanese convoy HI 72, which had sailed from Singapore, bound for Japan, on September 6, 1944. The convoy carried raw materials, a number of Japanese soldiers, several civilians, and 2,218 British and Australian prisoners of war.

Two U.S. submarine wolfpacks were on patrol in the South China Sea the night of September 12 when Ben's Busters (USS *Sealion*, USS *Growler*, and USS *Pampanito*) engaged the convoy. ULTRA had led them there.

One night, that silvery phosphorescent plankton saved the crew's lives. Lookout Tony Hauptman saw two silvery arrows coming right at the sub. He shouted the alarm: "Torpedoes!" The officer of the deck ordered the helm put hard right, and the torpedoes missed. They never saw the Japanese submarine: It was like two blind men fighting.

The *Pampanito* patrolled the coast for a month, diving by day and surfacing at night. The days are long in the Japanese summer, and the nights are short. Sometimes the crew could see bright lights on shore. When they were close to Tokyo Bay, crewman Elmer Smith remembers, they could see Mount Fuji, the snow-capped volcano sacred to the Japanese. "We took bearings off Fuji," Smith said. "We navigated by it."

They sighted a convoy in early July and attacked. More depth charges. Perhaps it was bad luck more than anything, but the second war patrol was not productive and on July 17, Summers headed the *Pampanito* back to Midway. She got there on July 23.

The Third Patrol: **Attack and Rescue in the South China Sea**
(August 17 to September 28, 1944)

The boat sailed again on August 17, this time in the company of two other boats—the *Growler* and the *Sealion*. This was the *Pampanito's* first wolfpack. The senior skipper and in command was Thomas Benjamin Oakley, Jr. in the USS *Growler*. The pack was named Ben's Busters and it was heading for the waters between Formosa—now called Taiwan—and the northern Philippine island of Luzon. This area of the ocean was called Convoy College, where submariners would earn advanced degrees in destruction.

It was on this patrol that the *Pampanito* would have her rendezvous with destiny.

The *Pampanito* had been on two long patrols by that summer, had stalked the enemy, had been attacked and nearly lost, and had brought the war within sight of Japan. She was lucky to have survived—but she was unlucky, too. It had been just over five months since the *Pampanito's* first patrol and she had yet to sink an enemy ship. The Navy wanted results.

Another wolfpack was in the Convoy College area—the submarines *Barb*, *Queenfish*, and *Tunny*. It was called Ed's Eradicators after Commander Edwin Swinburne, the senior officer.

On the trip west, the *Pampanito* had more bad luck: equipment problems and Japanese air patrols. Other subs spotted Japanese ships and called in the wolfpacks, but somehow the *Pampanito* missed the word. Then the submarine developed a leak up forward that had to be repaired at sea. The boat was spotted and bombed at least once off the coast of Luzon Island but escaped without further damage. Ben's Busters attacked a convoy, but the *Pampanito*, twisting and turning in pursuit of the enemy, never got off a shot.

Then came a secret message: A big convoy was heading up the South China Sea, not far from Hainan Island.

On September 12, the wolfpack converged on the convoy. The *Growler* fired first, sinking one of the ships. The *Sealion* fired and hit two ships, one of them the 9,400-ton transport ship *Rakuyo Maru* carrying Japanese troops and passengers. Again, the *Pampanito* was not in position to fire.

Then the convoy disappeared. But as the day turned into night, radar man George Moffett picked up a blip on the radar: It was the convoy, heading due north at a distance of seventeen miles. There were eight ships remaining in the convoy: four merchant ships and four Imperial Navy escorts. When all seemed lost, Moffett, who was one of the best radar men in the business, had saved the day.

At 10:40 that night, the *Pampanito* was finally in a position to fire. Summers fired five torpedoes from the forward tubes, swung the boat around, and fired four more from the after tubes.

It took four minutes for the torpedoes to reach their targets. Two of them hit the transport *Kachidoki Maru*. She was 525 feet long and displaced 10,500 tons, a big ship by the standards of

the day. Once the American ship *President Harrison*, whose home port was San Francisco, she had been captured by the Japanese in the first week of the war. One torpedo hit the *Kachidoki Maru* midship, one aft. It was a mortal blow; the engines stopped immediately and the ship started to sink by the stern, the bow rising higher and higher.

The convoy was in chaos; the *Pampanito* had hit yet another ship, a tanker, and it was burning.

On the *Kachidoki Maru*, there was panic, shouting, and screaming. The Japanese crew swung out the lifeboats and abandoned ship. The ship had been carrying about 1,300 passengers, including some wounded Japanese soldiers, who had no chance to get off. A Japanese officer went around with a pistol, shooting the wounded.

The main cargo, though, was British prisoners of war, 900 of them in the number-two hold, forward. They were being taken to Japan as slave labor on ships like this—hell ships, they called them.

Many of the prisoners were sick and dying. People were on deck yelling, "Over the side! Jump! Jump!" The bow rose higher and higher; an Allied officer, a prisoner, shouted that the ship was going: every man for himself. These men had seen war, had been prisoners for years, slaves, nearly; but this was the most terrifying thing

Left, full page: Survivors of the *Rakuyo Maru* are brought alongside the *Pampanito* during the rescue effort, September 15, 1944. Their "raft" is actually a hatch cover from the ill-fated ship. (U.S. Navy photograph by Paul Pappas)

Left, inset: Survivors on makeshift rafts reach the *Pampanito*. (U.S. Navy photograph by Paul Pappas)

Above: *Pampanito* crewmen gently lay a rescued man on the deck after plucking him from the South China Sea. The former prisoners were all in a weakened state after years of captivity and three days adrift with little or no food and water. (U.S. Navy photograph by Paul Pappas)

they had ever experienced. "This is it," thought George Hamilton, "This is the end of the road." The ship sank in fifteen minutes.

By this time, the *Pampanito* had surfaced and Summers was on the bridge, watching the Japanese ships burn and sink. At nearly 11:00, a bomb dropped close by and Summers decided to move away. In the distance, the submarine's lookouts could see gun flashes and tracers. A small escort vessel was sighted and Summers fired three torpedoes. They all missed. The *Pampanito*'s crew was exhausted—the skipper had been up for at least twenty-four hours straight. The boat submerged and left the area.

Rescued men await transfer to land at Saipan. The first man rescued, Australian Frank Farmer, stands in the foreground. (U.S. Navy photograph)

Aboard the *Kachidoki Maru*, some 400 Japanese passengers were killed but only 12 members of the crew. Of the 900 prisoners of war, 520 survived and were eventually picked up by the Japanese.

Three days went by; the *Pampanito* was patrolling on the surface, heading east from Hainan. The boat was deep in hostile waters, looking for remnants of the convoy. On the afternoon of September 15, one of the lookouts saw two rafts on the horizon, with men on board.

They were Japanese, Summers thought. Small arms were broken out, "and preparations were made for taking prisoners," Summers wrote in his report.

They were not Japanese; they were Australian and British prisoners, a handful of survivors left from the sinking of the *Rakuyo Maru*, torpedoed by the *Sealion* on September 12. The Japanese survivors had been picked up, but almost all of the prisoners were left to die. Some who tried to get aboard the Japanese rescue ships were driven off with clubs and rifle butts.

At first they sang. They sang "Rule Britannia" and "Land of Hope and Glory." But there was no glory and almost no hope. Slowly the shipwrecked men died, went mad, gave up, drifted off in the blistering sun.

"For three nights and four days, I was afloat on the open ocean with no water or food, covered with oil," said K. C. Renton, a soldier from Melbourne. "We were many miles from land, and it looked like the end. . . . On the fourth day, we began to get a bit dippy. . . . Some of them threw themselves over the side [of the raft]. They had been drinking seawater.

"That afternoon between four and five o'clock a marvelous and wonderful thing happened. A submarine was making straight for us. We did not know to whom it belonged. My eyes were paining with oil, and I could not see clearly, but when it was right opposite I saw a couple of men with a machine gun pointing at us. I didn't care because it would have been a quicker way out. . . ."

The *Pampanito*'s people were suspicious: A raft was sometimes a decoy for an enemy vessel lurking around, and everyone on the rafts was yelling and waving. There was no telling what these oil-covered scarecrows were saying. But it did sound like English.

Forty-six years after their rescue, Reg Bullock and Frank Farmer came all the way from Australia to visit the USS *Pampanito* in San Francisco in 1990. (SFMNPA photograph by Russell Booth)

One of the men, an Australian the others called Curly, had fair hair. The Americans were intrigued. The shouting went on: "First you bloody Yanks sink us," one man yelled, "now you're going to shoot us." Summers was still not sure; it could still be a trick. He told Tony Hauptman, the seaman on the bow with the gun, to take one—just one—aboard.

The man was an Australian soldier named Frank Farmer. He was helped up the side. "Thank you," he said. They took him to Lieutenant Commander Landon "Jeff" Davis, the executive officer. Farmer told Davis who the men were: Australian and British prisoners of war. Shipwreck survivors. The men on the *Pampanito*'s bridge were stunned, amazed. "Take them aboard," ordered Summers.

The men were wrecks, covered with oil, sick. Some of them couldn't see. The *Pampanito* men took them in, washed them off, put them in their bunks. The submarine was always crowded, but now she took on seventy-three more men, fed them, and took care of them.

The submarine carried no doctor, and it was before the age of paramedics. But there was Pharmacist's Mate First Class Maurice Demers, who was the next best thing. Everybody called him "Doc." He cared for the men. Later it was determined that 95 percent of the rescued prisoners had malaria at one time or another, 67 percent had recurrent dysentery, 61 percent had topical ulcers, and 9 out of 10 had some vitamin or nutritional deficiency.

"Their eyes were like dead men's eyes, dim, lifeless, as though they had lost everything but their souls," Demers remembered. "As I examined and treated each one, I could feel a deep sense of gratitude, yet their faces were expressionless and only a few could move their lips to whisper a faint 'thanks.' "

They had been given back their lives; it seemed incredible, some kind of miracle; they were

Above left: Survivors on *Pampanito*'s deck preparing for transfer at Saipan give a heartfelt "thumbs up" for their treatment on board during the five-day journey from the South China Sea. (National Archives, 80-G-284523)

Above right: TEMPORARY CITATION FOR NAVY AND MARINE CORPS MEDAL TO PHARMACIST'S MATE MAURICE DEMERS. This original copy was carefully preserved and donated to the Maritime Park Association by "Doc" Demers' sons, Lawrence and Kevin. Signed by Admiral Nimitz, it commends Demers for his extraordinary role in the prisoner of war rescue. (SFMNPA Collection)

grateful in a way that was beyond gratitude. Only when the men told their stories did the *Pampanito* sailors find out why.

Some had fought in Java, they said, some in Malaya, some in Singapore, caught in the great disaster that had overtaken the British and Australians.

"To make a long story short," one said about the defense of Java, "we had no hope against the Japanese, and we could not escape the place. . . ." "It was hell on earth," said H.J. Barker, a private in the Fourth Royal Norfolk Regiment, who served in Singapore. "It was impossible to hold a front line without reinforcements and there were no reinforcements. . . . We waited for further orders. . . . The orders were to lay down our arms. . . ." He remembered his tough old colonel, weeping.

"The results were that we were Japanese prisoners of war," Barker said. "Later we learned that slaves would have been a much more appropriate word to have used."

K.C. Renton, an Australian, described how the men were taken to Burma for the construction of the Burma-Thailand railway. "There," he said, "our real troubles began."

Reggie Bullock, an Australian artillery man, told the *Pampanito* sailors that a man died for every cross tie on that railroad.

When it was finished, those who were still alive and fit enough were taken to Saigon in Indo-China (present-day Vietnam, Cambodia, and Laos) and told they would be shipped to Japan for more work. The ships were old, worn-out, and fetid. The holds into which the prisoners were forced were beyond description. And then, only a few days out of Singapore, the ships were attacked by American subs.

There were four days of unspeakable torture drifting on the ocean.

One of the rescued men died aboard the *Pampanito* and was buried at sea. But the prisoners, now on the American submarine, were free men once more. "Have you ever been a prisoner?" asked Frank Farmer. "If not, then you don't know what it is like to be free."

Summers asked the men to write down what they had to say. "I don't know how to put my feelings in words," said Renton, "but may God bless the captain and crew for the wonderful job they did in saving our lives and looking after us. There is not a man that will forget it."

The *Sealion* picked up fifty-four survivors, the *Barb* and *Queenfish* thirty-two more.

The Navy brass praised the *Pampanito*'s crew for "a splendid patrol." Summers got the Navy Cross. The shipwrecked prisoners got their lives back. Every September 15, the anniversary of the rescue, and until his death in 1996, Farmer sent a message to the staff at the *Pampanito* in San Francisco. "Ever since that day," he said many years later, "my favorite song has been 'Yankee Doodle.'"

The Fourth Patrol: **Fennomints** (October 28 to November 30, 1944)

The *Pampanito* sailed from Pearl Harbor on her fourth patrol in the last days of October 1944.

After more than seven months in the Pacific theater, the sleek gray boat was a veteran. She had been overhauled and repaired, and the men had been given liberty in Hawai'i. Summers was worn out after the third patrol—the one that involved the prisoner of war rescue—and needed a break. Captain Frank Fenno, the new skipper, was a confident and easy-going man.

The *Pampanito* sailed in company with three other boats, and since

Left: AUSTRALIAN NEWSPAPER ARTICLE. This article, which appeared in the November 18, 1944 edition of *The West Australian*, detailed the horrors endured by the prisoners of war. (SFMNPA Collection)

Above right: Captain Frank Wesley Fenno commanded the USS *Pampanito* on her fourth patrol in late 1944. (U.S. Navy photograph)

SKIPPERS

The *Pampanito* had four captains. Charles Jackson, who commissioned the boat and took her to Pearl Harbor, was relieved before the sub went into combat. Pete Summers served the longest. He'd made seven patrols before taking command of the *Pampanito*, and he made five more as skipper there. Frank Fenno, a full captain with four stripes, took the boat on the fourth patrol and did so well that he was awarded the Bronze Star. Last, Donald Scherer commanded the *Pampanito* for six months, seeing the boat through a major overhaul and her return to Pearl Harbor at war's end.

Fenno was a crew favorite. Summers was not. Pete Summers could be abrupt and solemn, but most of all he was cautious. The crew, young and eager, didn't appreciate Summers' careful approach to attacking enemy shipping. "In an attack, it isn't the young men who are scared," said Joe Senft, who sailed aboard the USS *Threadfin*. "It's the men with five or six patrols." Summers made a dozen patrols in World War II and was captain for five of them. On patrol he often slept on a tiny cot in the conning tower.

He had all of the responsibility, and it weighed on him. "You may not like him," said Elmer Smith, "but he brought us back. You can't knock him for that."

But was he a good skipper? "I'm standing here talking to you," Smith said years later. "So he can't be all bad."

Summers stayed in the Navy after the war, made captain and retired as a rear admiral. He died in 1993.

Pampanito skipper Lt. Comdr. Paul E. ("Pete") Summers surveys the transfer of survivors at Saipan, September 20, 1944. Although the skipper was often referred to as "the old man," Summers had celebrated his 31st birthday at sea only two weeks earlier. (U.S. Navy photograph)

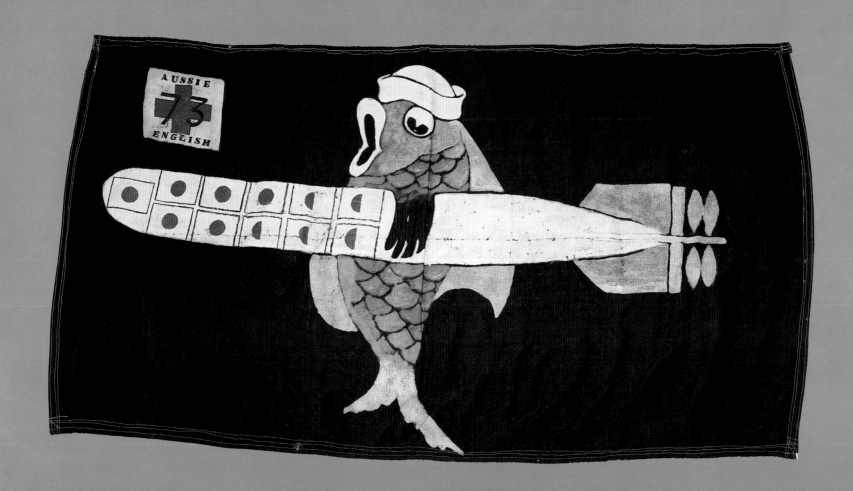

EARLY HAND-PAINTED BATTLEFLAG. Submarine battleflags were designed and created by the crew during patrols. This flag depicts a record of six ships sunk and five damaged. Often, damage claimed by submarines could not be verified after the war, and the records of many boats were revised downward. (SFMNPA Collection)

Fenno was senior, he took command of the wolfpack. The pack was called Fennomints—one of those wartime jokes—a play on Fenno's name and a brand of laxative popular back in the States.

The patrol area was deep in enemy waters, just off the China coast, and on the night of November 18, the subs closed in on a convoy. The weather was terrible, the seas so rough that Fenno fired six torpedoes at a single ship, the freighter *Shinko Maru*. Two hit. There was a bright flash and a huge column of black smoke. The *Shinko Maru* simply disappeared.

Several days later, another convoy, another attack, but no luck. Fenno used his subs to hunt and probe, catching yet another convoy and sinking several ships. By this time the seas were huge. The *Pampanito* had to be careful in surface attacks, lest she veer out of control.

The *Pampanito* was attacked by an escorting warship, was depth charged, but escaped again. At this point, the boat was running short of fuel, so Fenno turned command of the pack over to another skipper and set sail south, for Australia.

She sailed through the Japanese-held islands of Indonesia, though the narrow Lombok Strait west of Bali, and arrived in Fremantle, Western Australia, on December 30.

There the sub was met by some of the ex-prisoners she had rescued: a wonderful reunion. The Fennomints had done so well that Fenno himself was awarded the Bronze Star. For the crew, the reward was shore leave in Australia, a country of friendly people and strong beer. In the middle of the war, they thought they were in submarine heaven. But there was still more deadly work to do.

Above: BEER HALL PASS. This card, granting access to the submarine base beer hall, was issued to Torpedoman's Mate Elmer Smith, possibly while the sub was being refitted in Fremantle, Western Australia, after the fourth patrol. (SFMNPA Collection)

NEPTUNE CERTIFICATE AND SHELLBACK CARD. Crew members crossing the equator for the first time were initiated through a secret shipboard ceremony that turned them from inexperienced "polliwogs" into trusty "shellbacks." Summers even recorded such a ceremony in a patrol report: "Crossed the Equator. Found five polliwogs on board who had entered the Realm of Neptunus Rex without being initiated. Took necessary steps to remedy this situation." (SFMNPA Collection)

The Fifth and Sixth Patrols: **Mission Accomplished**

(January 23 to February 12, 1945 and February 25 to April 24, 1945)

Summers took the *Pampanito* out on her fifth patrol, this time in command of a two-sub wolfpack, with USS *Guavina*. They sailed north from Australia on January 23, 1945, through the Java Sea, and patrolled off the coast of Malaya. The *Pampanito* sank the 7,000-ton tanker *Engen Maru*, carrying fuel oil, rubber, and copper, and the passenger cargo vessel *Eifuku Maru*, which blew up with a huge explosion. But an escorting warship took off after the *Pampanito*, firing guns at her. Summers shrewdly conned his vessel and made off in the darkness, undamaged.

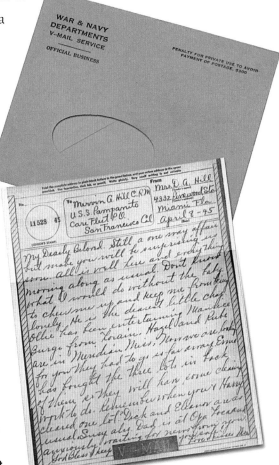

The boat was sent to Subic Bay in the Philippines, recently liberated from Japanese control. She sailed again in February, this time for the Gulf of Siam.

By this time, the American subs had worked their way out of a job: The *Pampanito* sank no ships on the sixth patrol; none were even sighted. The highlight of the trip was a rendezvous at sea with the USS *Sea Robin*, which had mail for the *Pampanito's* crew: It was the

V-MAIL RECEIVED BY CHIEF RADIOMAN MERVIN HILL. V-Mail was introduced to help handle the increased volume of mail during World War II. Letters written on specially designed 8½" x 11" stationery were photographed, the original destroyed, and the film flown overseas, where it was developed. The letter was delivered to the recipient in the form of a 4" x 5" photograph. (SFMNPA Collection)

0029 Had just about checked off three misses when the first torpedo hit, and simultaneously the ship disintegrated with the bow going one way, the stern in the opposite direction, and most of the ship going straight up. Judging from the intense flames and explosions, this ship was evidently loaded with aviation gasoline. One escort was close enough, I'm sure, to share in the effects of the explosions. The second torpedo probably hit whatever was left to hit. The whole area looked like a Fourth of July celebration, and we felt slightly naked in all this gaslight. Escort on starboard quarter commenced firing at us and placed several rounds just over the bridge before we could pull clear on all four main engines. For the next twenty minutes, one violent explosion followed another as the ship was torn to pieces. The stern sank, and the bow put on the finishing touch by exploding beautifully and in Technicolor.

Christmas mail, finally delivered in March.

Still, nothing. On April 5, the *Pampanito* pulled into Saipan for fuel, then sailed for Pearl Harbor. She arrived there on April 24 and soon moved on to San Francisco for an overhaul. She sailed under the Golden Gate Bridge on May 3 and went to Hunters Point Navy Yard.

The work took two months. Under Commander Donald Scherer, a new skipper, the *Pampanito* sailed out of the Golden Gate. The crew thought their next mission would be to support the invasion of Japan, but that never happened. While the *Pampanito* was at Pearl Harbor, Japan agreed to Allied surrender terms.

The *Pampanito's* record was good: six patrols, six ships sunk, four damaged, seventy-three former prisoners of war saved from certain death. Fifty-two American submarines had been lost, but the *Pampanito* went off to the fiercest war ever fought and came back. None of her crew was killed; they would live to see their grandchildren, live to see their experience become history. Some of them told their children long war stories. Some of them never talked about it. But they were marked for life by their experience in the war.

The *Pampanito* was sent back to San Francisco; she made her 697th and last dive off California on September 4, 1945. She was under for only fifteen minutes. In company with nine other submarines, she sailed into San Francisco Bay the next day, under the Golden Gate Bridge, past the city rising white and shining on its hills, past Pier 45, past the old gray Ferry Building, under the Bay Bridge, and on to Hunters Point. A sign on one of the piers said it all: "Welcome Home. Well Done."

BATTLE SCENE ILLUSTRATION. Color illustration of the *Pampanito* sinking an enemy vessel by I.R. Lloyd Studios, Vallejo, California. (SFMNPA Collection)

LETTERS SENT BY MURIEL I. MIX TO HER FUTURE HUSBAND, O.D. HAWKINS, WHILE HE WAS SERVING ON BOARD THE *PAMPANITO.* **Inspired by the "pin-up girl" artwork on military aircraft, Muriel, an art student in Minnesota, began illustrating the correspondence she sent overseas. In addition to writing to a brother and a cousin serving in the military, Muriel sent more than 300 letters to O.D. during the war, each with a unique illustration on the envelope.** (Courtesy of Muriel I. and O.D. Hawkins)

Above: **"CHEZ PAREE" SOUVENIR PHOTO. This photo was taken in May 1945 while the _Pampanito_ was in San Francisco for an overhaul. In the style of the day, the photo was taken professionally in a night club and mounted in a souvenir cover.** (SFMNPA Collection)

Right: **LETTER WRITTEN ABOARD THE _PAMPANITO_ ON SEPTEMBER 3, 1945. This letter, written by Radioman Thomas Lawson, apparently never was mailed and was found in the _Pampanito's_ radio room in 1982.** (SFMNPA Collection)

Left: The crew posed for this photograph shortly after the end of the war in September 1945, in San Francisco. (Photo source unknown)

PAMPANITO

73

Epilogue

The *Pampanito* was decommissioned on December 15, 1945, at Mare Island Navy Yard. Lieutenant Charles Bartholomew—Black Bart, they called him—was on board when the flag was hauled down. "I put her in decommission," he said. "It was the hardest job I ever had."

But the boat did not die. She became a reserve training sub at Mare Island in 1960. She never sailed again. In December 1971, she was stricken from the Navy rolls.

As a memorial, she is still alive. Every year nearly 200,000 visitors come aboard and see the submarine, thinking, wondering what it was like to serve aboard her. The *Pampanito* is also a classroom, a teaching tool about the war and the people who fought in it. On many nights, young boys and girls come and spend the night on the boat, sleeping where the crew slept, feeling the slow roll of the San Francisco Bay, listening to the sounds the saltwater makes. Sometimes, it feels as if the old boat was about to put out to sea again—that the spirit of those wartime sailors is still there.

The pull of those days is strong. George Ingram had not seen the *Pampanito* for fifty-five years when he walked up the apron at Pier 45 for a crew reunion one bright November day in 2000. "When I saw that boat," he said, "tears came to my eyes. When I went aboard, I kissed the deck."

The decommissioning party in December 1945 provided this opportunity to show off the *Pampanito* battleflag. (Photo source unknown)

Acknowledgments

The information in this book came from a number of sources, including histories of World War II and the submarine service.

Particularly valuable was Greg Michno's account of the *Pampanito, USS* Pampanito: *Killer Angel.* Michno's father served aboard the sub during World War II.

The wartime Patrol Reports and Deck Logs of the *Pampanito,* plus unpublished narratives of the rescued British and Australian prisoners of war in the archives of the San Francisco Maritime National Park Association, were consulted.

Surviving members of the *Pampanito*'s wartime crew were interviewed at the crew reunion in the fall of 2000. There were also interviews with the late Frank Farmer and Reggie Bullock, Australian prisoners of war, during their visit to San Francisco in 1990.

The assistance of *Pampanito* Ship's Manager Chris Bach, Assistant Manager Tom Richardson, and Curator Aldona Sendzikas was invaluable. The inspiration and hard work of the late Russell Booth, who managed the *Pampanito* as a memorial at Pier 45 in San Francisco for many years, is beyond praise.

Select Bibliography

Alden, John D. *The Fleet Submarine in the U.S. Navy*. Annapolis: Naval Institute Press, 1979.

Blair, Clay, Jr. *Silent Victory: The U.S. Submarine War Against Japan*. Philadelphia and New York: J.B. Lippincott Company, 1975.

Blair, Clay, Jr. and Joan Blair. *Return from the River Kwai*. New York: Simon and Schuster, 1979.

Costello, John. *The Pacific War*. New York: Rawson, Wade Publishers, Inc., 1981.

Enright, Joseph F. *Shinano! The Sinking of Japan's Secret Supership*. New York: St. Martin's Press, 1987.

Jane's Fighting Ships of World War II. New York: Military Press, 1989.

Michno, Gregory F. *USS* Pampanito*: Killer-Angel*. Norman, OK: University of Oklahoma Press, 2000.

National Maritime Museum Association *Sea Letter,* 35 (Winter 1984/85), 36 (Summer 1985), 37 (Spring 1987), and 51 (Spring 1996).

Roscoe, Theodore. *United States Submarine Operations in World War II*. Annapolis: United States Naval Institute, 1949.

Rush, C.W., W.C. Chambliss and H.J. Gimpel. *The Complete Book of Submarines*. Cleveland: The World Publishing Company, 1958.

Werner, Herbert A. and Edward L. Beach. *Iron Coffins: A Personal Account of the German U-Boat Battles of World War II*. New York: Holt, Rinehart and Winston, 1969.

Wheeler, Keith. *War Under the Pacific*. Alexandria, VA: Time-Life Books, 1980.

Winslow, Richard E., III. *Portsmouth-Built: Submarines of the Portsmouth Naval Shipyard*. Portsmouth, NH: The Portsmouth Marine Society/Peter E. Randall, 1985.

The Crew

**Officers And Men At Commissioning
November 6, 1943**

Officers

Lt. Comdr. Charles Barzzelious
Jackson, Jr., Commanding Officer
Lt. Comdr. Paul Edward Summers,
Executive Officer and Navigator
Lieut. Landon Leslie Davis,
Engineering and Electrical Officer
Lieut. William Harrison McClaskey, Jr.,
Torpedo and Gunnery Officer,
Construction and Repair Officer,
and Commissary Officer
Lieut. Clifford Charles Grommet,
Assistant Engineering and Electrical
Officer, Assistant Construction & Repair
Officer, Assistant Commissary Officer
Lt. (jg) Francis Michael Fives,
Communications Officer
Machinist James Samuel Heist,
Assistant Engineering and
Electrical Officer

Enlisted

Agnello, Lewis Jerry S1c
Aimone, Otto Peter, Jr. EM3c
Arcement, Norman John EM3c
Attaway, Ralph Winston EM1c
Bacskay, Albert Joseph SM3c
Baron, Leonard TM2c
Bennett, Robert TM3c
Bienkowski, Chester Charles F1c
Bobb, Louis Edward S1c

Boozer, James Steadman F2c
Bouchard, Jacques Florian S2c
Branch, Lamont F1c
Brown, George Valentine CEM
Brown, Hubert Nelson S1c
Connelly, William Guy S2c
Cordon, Walter Harold EM3c
Costello, Irving Francis MoMM2c
Cox, James Elton SC1c
Currier, Andrew Louis F2c
Davenport, Bartlett Nathaniel EM2c
De Buono, Juagindo F1c
Eichner, Joseph Frederick S2c
Ferguson, Donald Innes S1c
George, Howard Edwin TM1c
Glazik, Henry John MoMM2c
Grady, William Christopher MoMM1c
Hauptman, Anthony Carl GM2c
Herber, Ralph Monroe RM3c
Hill, Mervin RM1c
Hill, Samuel Richard CSM
Hopper, Gordon Lewis S2c
Kaup, Norbert Anthony MoMM2c
King, Theodas Cowen Cox
Kordich, Nickolas S2c
Kubacki, Edwin MoMM1c
Langin, Lawrence Harold EM1c
Lederer, Frank Joseph TM2c
Lombardi, Renard Joseph S2c
McVane, Lloyd Vivian F2c
Madaras, John George MoMM2c
Matheny, Robert Joseph TM1c
McGuire, Charles Albert, Jr. Y1c

Merryman, William Walter MoMM1c
Meyers, Milton Alfred QM3c
Michno, Frank Ben MM1c
Moffett, George Edward RT2c
Moore, Melvin Henry CMoMM
Morrow, William Franklin, Jr. SC3c
Mosey, Ray George EM1c
O'Neill, John Bernard PhM1c
Pappas, Paul, Jr. EM2c
Partridge, Leland Root CMM
Penn, Leonard Thomas TM2c
Rahner, Harold Joseph CTM
Robinson, Isaac Frederick TM3c
Schilling, John Beveridge QM1c
Smith, John Franklin StM2c
Smith, Wendall Tyng MoMM2c
Stinson, Harry MoMM1c
Thaxton, O'Neal St1c
Tonkin, Edward Martin S2c
Van Atta, Albert Dillon, Jr. S1c
Vaughan, Ishamel Worth RM2c
Watkins, Earl Finley MoMM2c
Weaver, Woodrow Wilson TM1c
Wilkerson, Jack Roslyn EM2c
Wilson, John Edward F2c
Zalusky, Bernard TM3c

**First War Patrol
March 15 - May 2, 1944**

Officers

Lt. Comdr. Paul Edward Summers,
Commanding Officer
Lieut. Landon Leslie Davis, Jr.,
Executive Officer and Navigator

Lieut. William Harrison McClaskey, Jr.,
    Engineering and Electrical Officer
Lieut. Clifford Charles Grommet,
    First Lieutenant
Lt. (jg) Edward Joseph Hannon, Jr.,
    Torpedo and Gunnery Officer
Lt. (jg) William Lee Bruckart,
    Radar Officer
Lt. (jg) Francis Michael Fives,
    Communications Officer
Ens. John West Red, Jr.,
    Commissary Officer
Machinist James Samuel Heist,
    Assistant Engineering Officer
Electrician Percy Bryan Pike,
    Assistant Electrical Officer

Enlisted

Agnello, Lewis Jerry TM3c
Aimone, Otto Peter, Jr. EM3c
Arcement, Norman John EM3c
Attaway, Ralph Winston EM1c
Austin, Joseph Charles Cave S1c
Bacskay, Albert Joseph SM2c
Baron, Leonard TM1c
Beaulieu, Laurent F1c
Behney, James Harris TM2c
Bennett, Robert TM2c
Bobb, Louis Edward S1c
Bouchard, Jacques Florian S1c
Bourgeois, Roger Norman MoMM3c
Branch, Lamont MoMM2c
Brown, Duncan S2c
Brown, Hubert Nelson S1c
Canty, William Stephen SM1c
Carmody, Clarence George MoMM2c
Chinn, Harold F1c

Cordon, Walter Harold EM3c
Costello, Irving Francis MoMM2c
Currier, Andrew Lewis F1c
Davenport, Bartlett Nathaniel EM2c
Eberhard, Robert Earl FC2c
Eichner, Joseph Frederick S2c
Ferguson, Donald Innes EM3c
George, Howard Edwin TM1c
Glazik, Henry John MoMM2c
Grady, William Christopher MoMM1c
Hauptman, Anthony Carl GM2c
Herber, Ralph Monroe RM3c
Hill, Mervin RM1c
Hopper, Gordon Lewis S1c
Ingram, George StM1c
Kaup, Norbert Anthony MoMM3c
King, Theodas Cowen, Jr. Cox
Kordich, Nickolas S1c
Kubacki, Edwin MoMM1c
Langin, Lawrence Harold EM1c
Large, Bonham Davis SC1c
Lederer, Frank Joseph TM2c
Lombardi, Renard Joseph S1c
MacVane, Lloyd Vivian S1c
Madaras, John George MoMM2c
Martin, Lynn Leonard MoMM1c
Matheny, Robert Joseph TM1c
McCollum, William Henry RM2c
McGuire, Charles Albert, Jr. Y1c
Merryman, William Walter MoMM1c
Meyers, Milton Alfred QM2c
Michno, Frank Ben MoMM1c
Moffett, George Edward RT1c
Moore, Melvin Henry CMoMM
Morrow, William Franklin, Jr. SC2c
Mosey, Ray George EM1c

O'Neill, John Bernard PhM1c
Pappas, Paul, Jr. EM2c
Payton, Albert, Jr. StM1c
Rahner, Harold Joseph CTM
Richter, Walter Herman S2c
Robinson, Isaac Frederick TM2c
Schilling, John Beveridge QM1c
Smith, Clarence Harrold CMoMM
Smith, Wendall Tyng, Jr. MoMM2c
Stockslader, Edmund William MoMM3c
Tonkin, Edward Martin S1c
Van Atta, Albert Dillon, Jr. S1c
Walters, Roger Marcellus RM3c
Watkins, Earl Finley MoMM2c
Weaver, Woodrow Wilson TM1c
Wilkerson, Jack Roslyn EM2c
Wilson, John Edward F1c
Yagemann, William Ferdinand FC3c
Zalusky, Bernard TM3c

Second War Patrol
June 3 – July 23, 1944

Officers

Lt. Comdr. Paul Edward Summers,
    Commanding Officer
Lt. Comdr. Landon Leslie Davis,
    Executive Officer
Lt. Comdr. Clifford Charles Grommet,
    First Lieutenant
Lieut. Howard Thomas Fulton,
    Assistant Engineering Officer
Lieut. McMillan Houston Johnson,
    Assistant First Lieutenant
Lieut. Ted Nier Swain,
    Torpedo and Gunnery Officer
Lt. (jg) William Lee Bruckart,
    Communications and Radar Officer

Lt. (jg) Francis Michael Fives,
  Engineering Officer
Lt. (jg) John West Red, Jr.,
  Commissary Officer
Ens. Percy Bryan Pike,
  Electrical Officer

Enlisted

Arcement, Norman John EM2c
Attaway, Ralph Winston CEM
Austin, Joseph Charles Cave TM3c
Bacskay, Albert Joseph SM2c
Bain, Cole Edward CMoMM
Baron, Leonard TM1c
Beaulieu, Laurent F1c
Behney, James Harris TM1c
Bennett, Robert TM2c
Bouchard, Jacques Florian S1c
Bourgeois, Roger Norman MoMM2c
Bowring, Harry Samuel MoMM3c
Branch, Lamont MoMM2c
Brown, Hubert Nelson TM3c
Byrd, Robert StM1c
Canty, William Stephen SM1c
Carmody, Clarence George MoMM2c
Chapman, Henry Roy F1c
Chinn, Harold MoMM3c
Cordon, Walter Harold EM3c
Costello, Irving Francis MoMM1c
Currier, Andrew Louis F1c
Davenport, Bartlett Nathaniel EM1c
Depray, Robert Francis F1c
Eberhard, Robert Earl FC2c
Eichner, Joseph Frederick SC3c
Evans, Jack Jay S1c
Ferguson, Donald Innes EM3c

George, Howard Edwin CTM
Grady, William Christopher MoMM1c
Hauptman, Anthony Carl GM1c
Herber, Ralph Monroe RM2c
Hill, Mervin CRM
Hopper, Gordon Lewis S1c
Ingram, George StM1c
Jansen, Kenneth James F2c
Kaup, Norbert Anthony MoMM1c
Kordich, Nickolas S1c
Langin, Lawrence Harold EM1c
Large, Bonham Davis CCS
Lederer, Frank Joseph TM2c
MacVane, Lloyd Vivian GM3c
Madaras, John George MoMM1c
Markham, Clyde Boyd MoMM3c
Martin, Lynn Leonard MoMM1c
McCollum, William Henry RM2c
McGuire, Charles Albert, Jr. Y1c
Merryman, William Walter CMoMM
Meyers, Milton Alfred QM2c
Michno, Frank Ben MoMM1c
Moffett, George Edward RT1c
Morrow, William Franklin, Jr. SC2c
Olive, Richard Hugh S1c
O'Neill, John Bernard PhM1c
Pappas, Paul, Jr. EM1c
Parris, Kyle Stanley S1c
Payton, Albert St3c
Richter, Walter Herman S2c
Robinson, Isaac Frederick TM2c
Schilling, John Beveridge QM1c
Scionti, Santo Sebastian MoMM3c
Smith, Clarence Harrold CMoMM
Smith, Wendall Tyng, Jr. MoMM1c
Smith, William Clyde F1c

Stimler, Spencer Hunt RT2c
Stockslader, Edmund William MoMM2c
Tonkin, Edward Martin TM3c
Van Atta, Albert Dillon, Jr. QM3c
Walters, Roger Marcellus RM2c
Weaver, Woodrow Wilson TM1c
Wilkerson, Jack Roslyn EM1c
Wilson, John Edward MoMM3c
Yagemann, William Ferdinand FC2c
Ylinen, Arthur F2c
Zalusky, Bernard TM3c

Third War Patrol
August 17 – September 28, 1944

Officers

Comdr. Paul Edward Summers,
  Commanding Officer
Lt. Comdr. Landon Leslie Davis, Jr.,
  Executive Officer and Navigator
Lt. Comdr. Clifford Charles Grommet,
  First Lieutenant
Lieut. Howard Thomas Fulton,
  Assistant Engineering Officer
Lieut. McMillan Houston Johnson,
  Assistant First Lieutenant
Lieut. Ted Nier Swain,
  Torpedo and Gunnery Officer
Lt. (jg) Francis Michael Fives,
  Engineering and Electrical Officer
Lt. (jg) John West Red, Jr.,
  Communications Officer
Lt. (jg) Richard James Sherlock,
  Radar Officer
Ens. Charles Kane Bartholomew,
  Commissary Officer

Enlisted

Arcement, Norman John EM2c
Austin, Joseph Charles Cave TM3c
Bacskay, Albert Joseph SM2c
Bain, Cole Edward CMoMM
Baron, Leonard TM1c
Beaulieu, Laurent F1c
Behney, James Harris TM1c
Bennett, Robert TM2c
Bixler, Herbert James SM3c
Bourgeois, Roger Norman MoMM2c
Bowring, Harry Samuel MoMM3c
Brown, Hubert Nelson TM3c
Byrd, Robert StM1c
Carmody, Clarence George MoMM2c
Chapman, Henry Roy F1c
Chichak, Andrew Frank FC3c
Chinn, Harold MoMM3c
Cordon, Walter Harold EM2c
Costello, Irving Francis MoMM1c
Currier, Andrew Louis F1c
Davenport, Bartlett Nathaniel EM1c
Demers, Maurice Lawrence PhM1c
Depray, Robert Francis F1c
Eichner, Joseph Frederick SC3c
Elkins, Kelly EM2c
Elliott, Allen Charles RM1c
Elliott, Richard Eugene MoMM3c
Evans, Jack Jay S1c
Evans, Robert Edward F1c
Ferguson, Donald Innes EM3c
Fisk, William Arthur MoMM2c
George, Howard Edwin CTM
Grady, William Christopher MoMM1c
Granum, Peder Anton TM3c

Greene, John Herman QM3c
Hauptman, Anthony Carl GM1c
Hayes, Daniel Edward SC2c
Herber, Ralph Monroe RM2c
Hill, Mervin CRM
Hopper, Gordon Lewis S1c
Ingram, George StM1c
Jansen, Kenneth James F2c
Kaup, Norbert Anthony MoMM1c
Kordich, Nickolas S1c
Lynch, Harry Steven EM3c
MacVane, Lloyd Vivian GM3c
Madaras, John George MoMM1c
Markham, Clyde Boyd MoMM3c
Martin, Lynn Leonard MoMM1c
McGuire, Charles Albert, Jr., Y1c
Mendez, Manuel Alfred S2c
Merryman, William Walter CMoMM
Moffett, George Edward RT1c
Morrow, William Franklin, Jr. SC2c
Olive, Richard Hugh S1c
Pappas, Paul, Jr. EM1c
Parris, Kyle Stanley S1c
Payton, Albert, Jr. St3c
Price, William Francis Y2c
Robinson, Isaac Frederick TM2c
Schilling, John Beveridge QM1c
Smith, Clarence Harrold CMoMM
Smith, Elmer William S1c
Smith, Wendall Tyng, Jr. MoMM1c
Smith, William Clyde F1c
Stimler, Spencer Hunt RT2c
Stockslader, Edmund William MoMM2c
Strother, George William S1c
Thompson, Herbert Earl CEM

Tonkin, Edward Martin TM3c
Van Atta, Albert Dillon, Jr. QM3c
Van Housen, Leroy Ellsworth S1c
Wanerman, Leonard RM3c
Weaver, Woodrow Wilson TM1c
Wilkerson, Jack Roslyn EM1c
Williams, Clarence EM3c
Wilson, John Edward MoMM3c
Yagemann, William Ferdinand FC2c
Ylinen, Arthur F2c

Fourth War Patrol
October 28 – December 30, 1944

Officers

Capt. Frank Wesley Fenno, Jr.,
    Commanding Officer
Comdr. Earl Twining Hydeman,
    Prospective Commanding Officer
Lt. Comdr. Landon Leslie Davis, Jr.,
    Executive Officer And Navigator
Lieut. Howard Thomas Fulton,
    Assistant Engineering Officer
Lieut. McMillan Houston Johnson,
    First Lieutenant
Lieut. Ted Nier Swain,
    Torpedo And Gunnery Officer
Lt. (jg) Francis Michael Fives,
    Engineering And Electrical Officer
Lt. (jg) John West Red, Jr.,
    Communications Officer
Lt. (jg) Richard James Sherlock,
    Radar Officer
Ens. Charles Kane Bartholomew,
    Commissary Officer

Enlisted

Arcement, Norman John EM2c
Austin, Joseph Charles Cave TM3c
Bacskay, Albert Joseph SM2c
Beaulieu, Laurent F1c
Behney, James Harris TM1c
Bennett, Robert TM2c
Bergfeld, Patrick Henry F1c
Bixler, Herman James SM3c
Bourgeois, Roger Norman MoMM2c
Bowring, Harry Samuel MoMM3c
Brown, Hubert Nelson TM3c
Bulceco, Rufino CCk
Butler, Stanley Freemont F1c
Carmody, Clarence George MoMM2c
Chichak, Andrew Frank FC3c
Chinn, Harold MoMM3c
Cordon, Walter Harold EM2c
Costello, Irving Francis MoMM1c
Crane, Travis Lee S1c
Currier, Andrew Louis EM3c
Davenport, Bartlett Nathaniel EM1c
Demers, Maurice Lawrence PhM1c
Depray, Robert Francis EM3c
Elkins, Kelly EM2c
Elliot, Allen Charles EM1c
Elliot, Richard Eugene MoMM3c
Evans, Robert Edward F1c
Ferguson, Donald Innes EM2c
Fisk, William Arthur MoMM1c
Goodson, John Evans F1c
Granum, Peder Anton TM3c
Greene, John Herman QM3c
Hauptman, Anthony Carl GM1c
Hawkins, Ona Denham F1c

Hayes, Daniel Edward SC2c
Higgins, Joseph John S1c
Hill, Mervin CRM
Hopper, Gordon Lewis S1c
Ingram, George St3c
Jansen, Kenneth James F1c
Johnson, John Lewis StM1c
Kaup, Norbert Anthony MoMM1c
Kordich, Nickolas RM3c
Madaras, John George MoMM1c
Madison, Walter Robert F1c
Markham, Clyde Boyd MoMM3c
Martin, Lynn Leonard MoMM1c
McGehee, Ervin Omer S1c
McGuire, Charles Albert, Jr. Y1c
Mendez, Manuel Alfred S1c
Merryman, William Walter CMoMM
Moffett, George Edward RT1c
Morrow, William Franklin, Jr. SC2c
Noker, Lawrence Edward F1c
Olive, Richard Hugh S1c
Pace, Charles Anthony F1c
Pappas, Paul, Jr. EM1c
Parris, Kyle Stanley S1c
Pennell, James Thomas, Jr. Y3c
Rechner, George Martin S1c
Redfield, Richard Wentworth S1c
Robinson, Isaac Frederick TM2c
Russell, Theodore Kenneth F1c
Smith, Clarence Harrold CMoMM
Smith, Elmer William S1c
Smith, William Clyde F1c
Stimler, Spencer Hunt RT1c
Stockslader, Edmund William MoMM2c
Strother, George William, Jr. S1c

Thompson, Herbert Earl CEM
Tonkin, Edward Martin TM3c
Van Atta, Albert Dillon, Jr. QM3c
Van Housen, Leroy Ellsworth S1c
Vitello, Donato Bkr1c
Walters, Roger Marcellus RM2c
Wanerman, Leonard RM3c
Weaver, Woodrow Wilson TM1c
Williams, Clarence EM3c
Wilson, John Edward MoMM3c
Wood, Paul Jackson S1c
Yagemann, William Ferdinand FC2c

Fifth War Patrol
January 23 – February 12, 1945

Officers

Comdr. Paul Edward Summers,
    Commanding Officer
Lt. Comdr. William Jack Bush,
    Prospective Commanding Officer
Lt. Comdr. Lynn Stanley Orser,
    Executive Officer
Lieut. McMillan Houston Johnson,
    First Lieutenant
Lieut. Ted Nier Swain,
    Torpedo and Gunnery Officer
Lieut. Francis Michael Fives,
    Engineering and Electrical Officer
Lt. (jg) John West Red, Jr.,
    Communications Officer
Lt. (jg) Richard James Sherlock,
    Radar Officer
Lt. (jg) Charles Kane Bartholomew,
    Commissary Officer
Ens. Edmund Eugene De Paul,
    Assistant Engineering Officer